Angels are spiritual beings that live in heaven with God.

Angels are messengers from God.

An angel of God loves Jesus.

An Angel of God speaks God's word.

An angel of God is full of love.

An angel of God is full of light that never fades away.

An angel of God protects little children.

The angels of God are full of smiles and happy faces. They are not scary or creepy.

An angel of God does not cause fear but will tell you, "Fear not."

An angel of God does no evil.

An angel of God speaks the truth.

The angels of God are very strong.

An angel of God is full of wisdom.

Angels of God sing praises to God all the time.

An angel of God delivers children from trouble.

An Angel of God guides little children.

Angels of God are obedient to God.

An angel of God heals little children when they are sick.

An Angel of God brings comfort.

An Angel of God fights for God's children.

Angels worship God.

Angels help little children.

Angels of the little children see the face of God in heaven.

Every child has a guardian angel. So, never feel that you are alone. Always know that God sent His angel to guide, protect and help you in your lifetime on earth.

The next time you see an angel, you'll know if he is from God or not.

See that you do not despise one of these little ones. For I tell you that their angels in heaven always see the face of my Father in heaven.

Matthew 18:10

www.ingramcontent.com/pod-product-compliance
Lightning Source LLC
Chambersburg PA
CBHW041447120626
46547CB00002B/384